KEYBOARD CHART

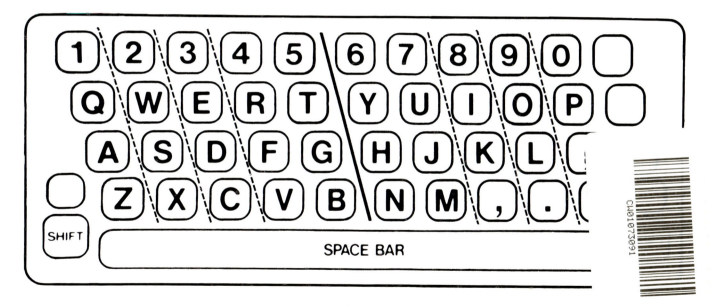

KEYPAD CHART

See page 49 for keypad instructions.

KEYBOARDING

Personal typing and information processing

Doreen Napper   Delia Craig

Pitman

Pitman Publishing
A division of
Longman Cheshire Pty Limited
Longman House
Kings Gardens
95 Coventry Street
Melbourne 3205 Australia

Offices in Sydney, Brisbane, Adelaide
and Perth. Associated companies, branches
and representatives throughout the world.

Copyright © D Napper, D Craig 1982, 1985
First published 1982
Reprinted 1983, 1984 (twice),
Second edition 1985
Reprinted 1987, 1988

All right reserved. Except under the conditions described
in the Copyright Act 1968 of Australia and subsequent
amendments, no part of this publication may be reproduced,
stored in a retrieval system or transmitted in any form
or by any means, electronic, mechanical, photocopying,
recording or otherwise without the prior permission of
the copyright owner.

Designed by Lynda Patullo
Produced by Pitman Publishing
Printed in Hong Kong

National Library of Australia
Cataloguing - in - Publication data

National Library of Australia
Cataloguing in Publication data

Napper, Doreen
Keyboarding.
ISBN 0 85896 237 3

1. Typing - Exercises, worked examples.
I. Craig D. II. Title.

652.3

Contents

Introduction

Part 1	Your machine	1
	Manual typewriter	1
	Electric typewriter	2
	Electronic typewriter	3
	Word processor	4
	Computer	5

Part 2	Preparing to key	6
	First steps	6
	Keying by touch	9
	Proof-reading	11

Part 3	The alphabetic and numeric keyboard	12
	Unit 1 Guide keys: asdf jkl;	13
	Unit 2 HE 3	15
	Unit 3 TI 58	18
	Unit 4 RN 4	21
	Unit 5 CO 9	24
	Unit 6 Full stop; shift keys	27
	Unit 7 YW 26	31
	Unit 8 GP 0	34
	Unit 9 UQ 17	37
	Unit 10 B comma	40
	Unit 11 MX	43
	Unit 12 VZ	46

Part 4	The numeric keypad	49
	Unit 13 Guide keys: 456	50
	Unit 14 71	51
	Unit 15 82	52
	Unit 16 93	53
	Unit 17 0 decimal point	54

Part 5	Signs and symbols	55
	Unit 18 Question mark, colon	56
	Unit 19 Hyphen, dash	57
	Unit 20 Parentheses, asterisk	58
	Unit 21 Apostrophe, quotation marks	59
	Unit 22 Exclamation mark, per cent	60
	Unit 23 Dollar sign, diagonal/solidus	61
	Unit 24 @, underscore	62
	Unit 25 &, minus sign	63
	Unit 26 Plus, division signs	64
	Unit 27 Multiplication, equal signs	65
	Unit 28 Metric, degree°	66
	Unit 29 Superior characters	67
	Unit 30 Roman numerals	68

| Part 6 | Paragraph drills | 69 |

| Part 7 | Passage drills | 75 |

Part 8	Production work	85
	Unit 31 Centring	86
	Unit 32 Letters and envelopes	87
	Unit 33 Correction marks	89
	Unit 34 Tables	92

| Part 9 | A computer program | 94 |

Introduction

This book presents a short and thorough course in learning to operate 'by touch' the standard keyboard found on manual, electric and electronic typewriters, as well as word processors and computers, and the keypad found on many computer terminals.
The book teaches the student to:
- identify the parts of the machine
- set up the machine
- key 'by touch'
- proofread
- operate the alphabetic, numeric, punctuation sign and symbol keys
- build accuracy and speed
- key from drafts and corrected copy
- centre material
- set out letters, envelopes and tables
- become familiar with word processing and computer vocabulary
- identify a computer program

In this revised edition of *Keyboarding*, the numeric keys have been introduced alongside the alphabetic keys; a method of learning that the authors advocate. However, if preferred, the numeric keys (which are on the C pages of each unit) may be learned following the alphabetic keys.

Also in this edition, the drill passages in part 7 have been revised to conform to the requirements of the Australian Standards Association for typing speed tests.

ACKNOWLEDGMENT

Much of the material used in the timed passages is taken from Bradbeer, De Bono & Laurie, *The Computer Book*, BBC, 1982.

1 Your machine

MANUAL TYPEWRITER

Although the manual typewriter has been superseded by the electric and electronic models, it is still the first machine on which many students learn to type.

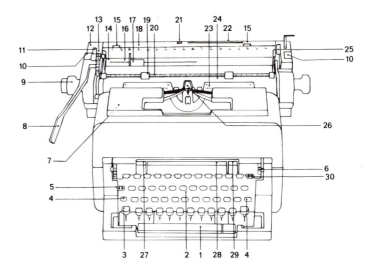

BASIC PARTS

1 Space bar
2 Keyboard
3 Shift key
4 Shift lock
5 Margin release key
6 Ribbon switch/stencil switch
7 Ribbon reverse levers
8 Carriage return lever/line space lever
9 Cylinder knob/platen knob
10 Carriage release control
11 Interlineator/automatic line finder
12 Carriage
13 Line space regulator
14 Paper tray
15 Margin stops
16 Paper edge guide scale
17 Paper edge guide
18 Margin scale
19 Paper bail and rolls
20 Paper bail scale
21 Paper support release
22 Paper support
23 Alignment scales
24 Cylinder/platen
25 Paper release lever
26 Type guide
27 Tab set key
28 Tab bar
29 Tab clear key
30 Backspace key

9 A computer program

Study the following computer program written in *BASIC programming language*.
It is the first part of a stock maintenance program.

```
100 PRINT "STOCK MAINTENANCE OPTIONS"
200 PRINT "SELECT ONE OF THE FOLLOWING"
300 PRINT "        1 FILE HEADER CHANGES"
400 PRINT "        2 ADDITIONS OF NEW ITEMS"
500 PRINT "        3 CHANGES TO EXISTING ITEMS"
600 PRINT "        4 PRICE & DISCOUNT CHANGES"
700 PRINT "ENTER REQUIRED SELECTION" : INPUT A
800 IF A=1 THEN GOTO 1200
810 IF A=2 THEN GOTO 1300
820 IF A=3 THEN GOTO 1400
830 IF A=4 THEN GOTO 1500
900 PRINT "INVALID SELECTION - TRY AGAIN"
920 GOTO 700
1200 PRINT "CHANGES TO FILE HEADER SHOULD ONLY"
1210 PRINT "BE CARRIED OUT AT MONTH-END AFTER"
1220 PRINT "ALL MONTHLY REPORTS ARE COMPLETED"
1230 GOTO 2000
1300 PRINT "ADDITIONS OF NEW ITEMS SHOULD BE"
1310 PRINT "ENTERED OFF A FORM 2A. THESE ARE"
1320 PRINT "ISSUED BY THE ORDER DEPARTMENT"
1330 GOTO 2200
1400 PRINT "USE FORM 2B TO CHANGE DETAILS ON"
1410 PRINT "EXISTING STOCK ITEMS"
1420 GOTO 2400
1500 PRINT "USE FORM 3A ISSUED BY MARKETING TO"
1510 PRINT "ALTER STOCK PRICES & DISCOUNTS"
1520 GOTO 2600
```

ELECTRIC TYPEWRITER

The electric typewriter has a number of features which make it faster and easier to operate than the manual. Its golf ball or daisy wheel typing element also provide more professional looking copy.

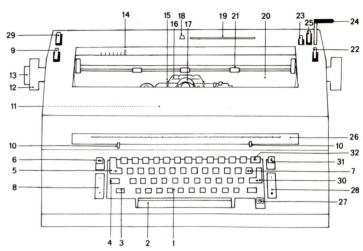

BASIC PARTS

1 Keyboard
2 Space bar
3 Shift key
4 Shift lock
5 Tab key
6 Margin release key
7 Express backspace key
8 Tab set/clear control
9 Half spacing selector
10 Margin stops
11 Ribbon switch/stencil switch
12 Cylinder knob/platen knob
13 Variable line spacer
14 Paper edge guide
15 Ribbon carrier
16 Alignment scales
17 Type element ('golf ball')
18 Paper support release
19 Paper support
20 Cylinder/platen
21 Paper bail and rolls
22 Interlineator/automatic line finder
23 Line space regulator
24 Paper injector/ejector
25 Paper release lever
26 Front scale/margin stop scale/pitch scale
27 Correction key
28 On/off switch
29 Pitch selector
30 Type element/carriage return key
31 Index key
32 Backspace key

Fourteen spaces have been left between the columns of figures.

WILLIAMS INTERIORS

Summary of merchandise ordered

Month: November

Stock number	Metres ordered	Price (metre) $	Total cost $
81644	12.50	23.25	219.63
81933	8.75	24.96	218.40
82377	16.25	24.56	399.10
82755	9.50	39.96	379.62
83244	15.00	7.96	119.40
83599	21.25	9.49	201.66
83777	17.75	18.46	327.67
84166	24.00	13.45	322.80

ELECTRONIC TYPEWRITER

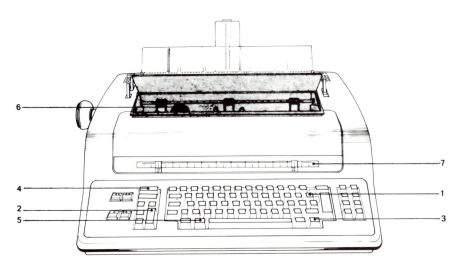

1 Decimal tab
2 Code key
3 Automatic return
4 Memory key
5 Repeat key
6 Printwheel
7 Visible display window

The electronic typewriter enables even greater speed and efficiency in keying than the electric typewriter. Features found on modern electronic typewriters include:

- Automatic functions such as margin setting, line spacing/carriage return, centring, decimal alignment, tabulation, underscoring, correction, right-hand justification of the text, paragraph indention and the ruling of vertical lines.
- Proportional spacing whereby more space is allowed for wide letters (such as 'm') and less space for narrow letters (such as 'l').
- Multilingual keyboard capability.
- A computer 'memory' which stores information such as frequently used headings, dates, salutations, letter endings, common phrases, and so on. It can also 'remember' page formats to enable easy production of pre-printed forms, or produce an unlimited number of 'original' copies of the same document.
- A visual display window which shows the characters just typed. A function of this display is to allow modifications to be made to the text before it is printed on the page.
- Performance of arithmetic functions such as addition, subtraction, multiplication and division.

UNIT 34 TABLES

Key the following tables using A5 paper. After the headings use the keypad (if provided on your machine) to key the numbers.

Fourteen spaces have been left between the columns of figures. Set a left hand margin stop for the first column and tab stops for the other columns according to the number shown at the head of each column.

STEVENS MANUFACTURING COMPANY

Production report for week ending 31 January 19--

10	29	48	67
Machine number	Total units produced	Hours in operation	Hourly production
21343	6 061	50.25	120.62
24447	8 336	65.75	63.75
37551	8 115	68.15	118.47
45678	4 921	59.75	83.26
46319	9 813	95.25	103.02
51426	8 381	66.5	126.03
55629	9 197	70.5	130.45

WORD PROCESSOR

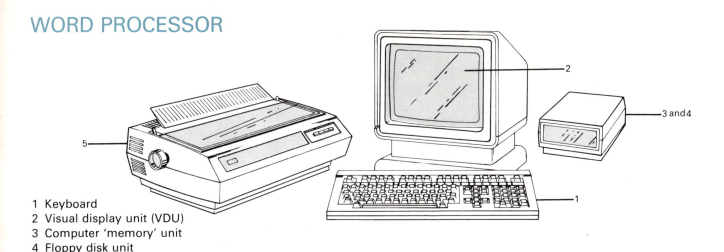

1 Keyboard
2 Visual display unit (VDU)
3 Computer 'memory' unit
4 Floppy disk unit
5 Printer

The word processor is an extension of the electronic typewriter. The major difference between word processors and electronic typewriters is their storage capability. Features found on word processors and additional to those found on electronic typewriters include:
- A full-screen visual display unit (VDU).
- Use of magnetic tapes, magnetic cards, floppy disks or diskettes for information storage.
- A unit for the printing of documents.
- Facilities for searching for or sorting stored files; deleting old information; renumbering and condensing old files; adding new records and printing out data on stored files.

Although machine features vary considerably, word processors may be divided into two major categories: stand alone word processors (each machine houses a micro-processing unit) which may have the facility to allow communication with other word processing machines, and shared-logic processors (a single micro-processor 'drives' the various devices connected to it such as individual workstations and printers). A word processor may have a keyboard and visual display unit combined, or a separate typewriter that functions as keyboard and printer (see illustration).

OPERATING THE SPACE BAR

Whether you are left-handed or right-handed, tap the space bar with the right-hand thumb.

More words begin and end with letters typed by the left hand than those typed by the right. by using your right-hand thumb for spacing, you have a balanced hand movement, which leads to better results. of course,

COMPUTER

A computer is an electronic device which can process and store large amounts of information. It can be described as a filing system of sorts.
   There are four basic parts to a computer: an input device, a memory, a central processor and an output device.
   The device by which information is usually entered into the computer is a keyboard similar to a typewriter keyboard but with additional keys used for specific functions.
   The printer is the most common device for computer output and output can be recorded at a very high speed.
   To process information (or data) the computer follows directions from the computer program. The computer program is devised by a person known as a computer programmer.
   A program is a series of commands which are expressed according to particular rules and specific symbols. (A sample program is on page 94; additional information on computers is contained in the passages beginning on page 76.)

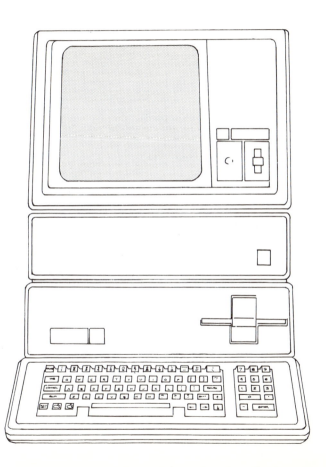

Courtesy of Electronic Concepts and Apple Computers

○ Key a corrected copy of the following two passages using A5 paper. Use margins of 10 (pica) and 18 (elite).

USING A DICTIONARY

A dictionary should be part of every keyboard operator's basic equipment. Whether you are doing work for yourself at home or whether you aim to be a top-level executive a dictionary is essential. [ds]
It should not be assumed that anyone is a perfect speller.

If your employer hands you a piece of work for keying, do not [s/s] take it for granted that there will be no contain mistakes in spelling. The final product will be your responsibility.

2 Preparing to key

FIRST STEPS
If you are using a manual or electric typewriter, follow these steps. If you are using an electronic typewriter, word processor or computer refer to the instruction manual.

Before you begin:

CENTRE THE CARRIAGE
On a machine with a carriage:
1 Locate the centre point of the paper bail scale.
2 Hold the cylinder knob and press down the carriage release control.
3 Move the carriage so that the typing point is at the centre of the carriage.
4 Release the carriage release control and the cylinder knob.

Note On a single-element electric machine with no carriage, use the space bar to centre the type element.

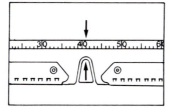

SELECT THE LINE SPACING
1 Locate the line space regulator.
2 Set the line space regulator at 1 for single line spacing.

Note When the regulator is set at 2, you will key in double line spacing, leaving one clear line space between keyed lines. When the regulator is set at 3, you will key in treble line spacing, leaving two clear lines of space between keyed lines. Many machines have intermediate settings such as 1½ and 2½.

ADJUST THE RIBBON SWITCH
1 Locate the ribbon switch.
2 Set the switch so that the top half of the ribbon is being used. This means that the switch is set at 'blue'.

INSERT AND STRAIGHTEN THE PAPER
1 Locate the: paper bail and rolls   paper edge guide scale
             paper bail scale   paper edge guide
             cylinder knobs   paper release lever
2 Pull the paper bail forward or up, away from the cylinder.
3 Set the paper edge guide at 0 on the paper edge guide scale.

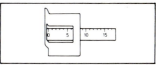

4 Holding the paper in your left hand, place the top edge of the paper behind the cylinder and the left-hand edge against the paper edge guide.

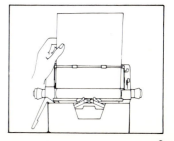

UNIT 33 CORRECTION MARKS

	MEANING
The typist who does not check work until after	Use single spacing
it has been removed # from the typewriter may waste	Leave a space
a lot of valuable time. If an er⌢ror is detected	Close up space
before the removal of / the paper, the correction	Insert a word, etc
will be simple to make.	Use double spacing
If, however, the error is not seen until later,	Begin a new paragraph
the reinsertion of the paper and ~~the~~ realignment	Let it stand (stet)
‖ of the typing with the aid of the alignment scales	Straighten the margin
and the variable line spacer will be	Run on
time-consuming.	
This is especially so when Carbon copies have	Use a small letter
been made. each copy must be altered separately.	Use a capital letter
The typist who aims to have all work ~~finished~~ completed in	Alter a word
the time shortest is a valuable employee.	Change the order

5 Holding the paper with your left hand, turn the right cylinder knob with your right hand to bring the paper into the machine.

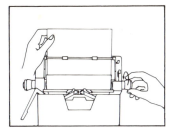

6 Check that the paper is straight by aligning the top and bottom edges or the left and right edges. Use the paper release lever to loosen the paper for straightening.

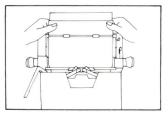

7 Replace the paper bail against the paper. Set the paper bail rolls so that there is approximately one-third of the width of the paper between them.

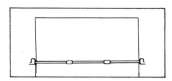

8 Check that the left-hand edge of the paper is on 0 on the paper bail scale. (This corresponds to the paper edge guide scale.)

FIND THE FIRST KEYING LINE

1 Locate the: alignment scales
                cylinder knobs
                paper bail
                line spacer/carriage return
2 Using the cylinder knob, turn the paper until the top edge is in line with the top edge of the alignment scales. Recheck alignment.
3 Lift the paper bail.
4 Using the line spacer/carriage return, turn down the required number of lines from the top of the paper.
5 Return the paper bail to its position against the cylinder.

SET THE MARGINS

Machines vary in the means of setting margin stops. Locate the margin stops on your typewriter.

MACHINE WITH A CARRIAGE
For machines with manual margin setting
1 Centre the carriage.
2 To set a left-hand margin, press the top of the left-hand margin stop while you slide the stop to the required point on the margin scale. Then release the stop.
3 To set a right-hand margin, press the top of the right-hand margin stop while you slide the stop to the required point on the margin scale. Then release the stop.

ENVELOPES

Key each of the following examples of envelopes. Start keying half way down the envelope and one-third of the way across.

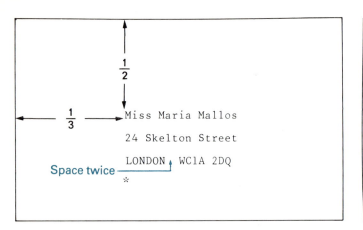
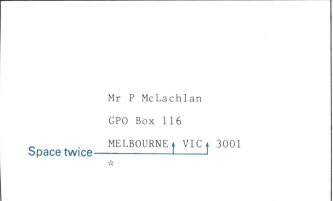
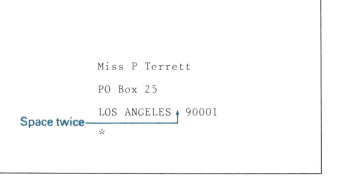

*When letters are sent from one country to another, the country of destination is typed on the envelope at this point (a double space below the last line of the address).

For machines with margin stops that are not visible

To set the *left-hand* margin:
1 Centre the carriage.
2 Move the carriage to the set left-hand margin. Press and hold the left-hand margin set key (or lever) as you move the carriage until the typing point is at the point at which you want to reset the margin. Release the key when you reach this point.

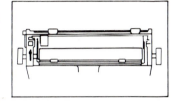

To set the *right-hand* margin:
1 Centre the carriage.
2 Move the carriage to the set right-hand margin. Press and hold the right-hand margin set key (or lever) as you move the carriage until the typing point is at the point at which you want to reset the right-hand margin. Release the key when you reach this point.

MACHINE WITH NO CARRIAGE
1 Centre the type element.
2 Set the left-hand and right-hand margin stops.

REMOVE THE PAPER
1 Locate the paper release lever.
2 Pull the paper release lever forward with the first finger of the right hand.
3 Keep your finger on the paper release lever as you remove the paper with your left hand.
4 Return the paper release lever to its original position immediately you have removed the paper.

UNIT 32 LETTERS AND ENVELOPES

A SAMPLE LETTER

Study the letter set out below and then key a copy using A5 paper and following the line spacing indicated. Use margins of 12 (pica) or 20 (elite). Commence on line six from the top of the sheet. Set the line space gauge for single spacing.

```
          80 Rose Avenue
          RYDE   NSW   2132
```
Space twice — Operate the line spacer/carriage return *twice*

```
          3 January 1985
```
Operate the line spacer/carriage return *three times*

```
          Messrs Dawson & Son
          26 Evans Crescent
          CROYDON   NSW   2132
```
Operate the line spacer/carriage return *twice*

```
          Dear Sirs
```
Operate the line spacer/carriage return *twice*

```
          Will you please send one of your employees to give me a
          quotation for landscaping the grounds of my new home at the
          above address.
```
Operate the line spacer/carriage return *twice*

```
          Any time between 9.30 am and 4.30 pm, Monday to Friday, will
          be convenient for me.
```
Operate the line spacer/carriage return *twice*

```
          Yours truly
```
Operate the line spacer/carriage return *four times*

```
          Rex Morrison
```

KEYING BY TOUCH

To key by touch is to operate the keyboard without looking at it.
- Operate the left-hand half of the keyboard with the left hand and the right-hand half with the right hand.
- Use the keys **A S D F** as guide keys for the left hand.
- Use the keys **J K L ;** as guide keys for the right hand.
- On a manual typewriter place the fingers of your left hand gently on the **A S D F** keys and the fingers of your right hand gently on the **J K L ;** keys. On an electric or electronic typewriter, word processor or computer keep your fingers just clear of the guide keys.
- Use the guide keys as a base from which to locate all other keys.
- After striking a key on another row, return the finger immediately to its guide key position.
- Operate the line spacer/carriage return without looking up.
- When keying, look at your copy—not at the keyboard.

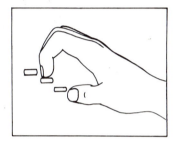

HANDS AND ARMS
- Curve your fingers
- Key with your fingertips
- Keep your thumbs close to the space bar
- Keep your wrists parallel with the slope of the keyboard
- Keep your arms relaxed and your elbows a little away from the sides of your body
- Do not rest your hands on the framework of the machine.

UNIT 31 CENTRING

Refer to the notes on centring on page 85 and centre the following material horizontally and vertically using A5 paper.

Set the line space regulator for single line spacing and operate the carriage return lever/return key according to the line spacing indicated.

Note:
Treble line spacing Operate the carriage return lever/return key three times. This gives two blank lines between the keyed lines.
Double line spacing Operate the carriage return lever/return key twice. This gives one blank line between the keyed lines.
Single line spacing Operate the carriage return lever/return key once.

		No of lines
	SPRINGBROOK GARAGE	1
Treble space		2
		3
	5-13 Norton Street	4
	Adelaide	5
Treble space		6
		7
	FOR REPAIR WORK OF EVERY DESCRIPTION BY	8
	EXPERT MECHANICS	9
Double space		10
	ALL WORK GUARANTEED	11

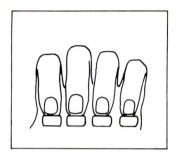

KEYSTROKING

- Keep hands, wrists and arms almost motionless
- Strike the keys with the fingertips
- Strike each key sharply in the centre
- Release each key quickly
- Move only one finger away from the guide key position at a time whenever possible
- Return each finger to the guide key position quickly.

SPACING

- Strike the space bar with the thumb of the right hand
- Strike the space bar with a sharp, short movement
- Space immediately after a word is typed.

LINE SPACING

On word processors, computers and some electronic typewriters new lines are started automatically.

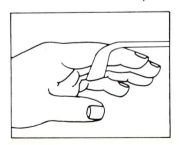

MANUAL MACHINES

- Keep your fingers curved naturally. Move the left hand quickly to the line spacer/carriage return
- Return the carriage firmly and swiftly with the side of the forefinger of the left hand
- Return the left hand quickly to the guide keys

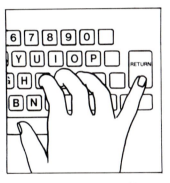

ELECTRIC/ELECTRONIC MACHINES

- Use the little finger of the right hand
- Keep the **J**, **K** and **L** guide key fingers in position
- Move the little finger quickly to the return key
- Lightly press the return key, release the key quickly and return the little finger to the guide key.

8 Production work

In this section you will apply the keyboarding skills developed in sections 1 to 7. At the same time you will learn the basic production skills required to:
- centre material horizontally and vertically
- format letters and envelopes
- interpret common correction marks
- lay out simple tables.

CENTRING MATERIAL

Use the following methods of centring material if operating a manual or electric typewriter. If you are using a word processor or computer, refer to the instruction manual.

VERTICAL CENTRING

A copy looks attractive if it is displayed in a central position. Vertical centring means that the top and bottom margins of a copy are equal. This is achieved by calculating the position of the first keying line so that the copy is centred vertically on the page.

Procedure

1. Count the number of lines that can be fitted on a page. This can be done by setting the line space regulator on '1' (single spacing) and operating the line spacer/carriage return.
2. Count the total number of lines (keyed and blank) within the material to be keyed. (Remember to count one blank line when the copy is double spaced and two blank lines when the copy is treble spaced.)
3. Subtract the number of lines to be keyed plus the number of blank lines from the total number of lines on the page. This will give the number of lines of space that are left.
4. Divide this space by two so that there will be equal margins above and below the material.
5. Begin keying on the next line below the top margin.

HORIZONTAL CENTRING

Horizontal centring means that the left- and right-hand margins of a copy are equal in width.

Procedure

1. Insert the paper into your machine with the left-hand edge at 0 on the paper bail scale.
2. Find the number of spaces that the paper will accommodate horizontally by measuring it across the paper bail scale. Half this number is the centre of the paper.
3. Position the printing point at the centre of the paper.
4. Backspace once for every second character or space in the line to be centred. If there is an odd number of characters, disregard the last character. (This will result in half the line being keyed to the left of the centre and half to the right of the centre.)
5. Begin keying at the point to which you have backspaced.

PROOF-READING

Proof-reading means locating and marking your errors. Develop skill in proof-reading by locating and marking errors in all your work.

PROCEDURE

1 Leave the completed copy in the machine.
2 Lift the paper bail from the copy and roll the paper up a few lines so that all lines can be read easily.
3 Read your copy carefully, one line at a time, circling any errors.
4 As you circle your errors, think about what you might have done to cause the error, and think about how you can avoid making the same error again.

For word processors and computers, proof-read the material on the visual display unit (VDU). Locate errors with the cursor and key the correct character.

Note the kinds of errors circled in the example below:

You must proof-read each (c opy)¹ before (itis)² removed from the machine.
Read (carefuly)³ as you circle (any)⁴ errors.
(Thinkk)⁵ about your errors as you circle (circle)⁶ them.
(T hink)⁷ about what you might have done to (c ause)⁸ each error.
Think how you (might)⁹ avoid making the same error (a gaim)¹⁰.

1 Extra space
2 Omitted space
3 Omitted letter
4 Omitted word
5 Extra letter
6 Extra word
7 Raised letter
8 Lowered letter
9 Overtype
10 More than one error in a word is counted as only one error.

11

SOME COMPUTER TERMS

```
           5|    10|   15|   20|   25|   30|   35|   40|   45|   50|   55|   60|   65|   strokes
```

'Data' is the information which a computer program deals   62
with. Data can be in the form of numbers or characters.   111

'Data processing' is the term used to describe the work for   170
which computers are used. Increasing numbers of businesses   229
are moving to electronic data processing of their accounts.   288

'Floppy disks' are flat magnetic disks on which programs and   348
data may be stored and from which information may be retrieved   410
quickly.   418

'Hardware' is the term used to describe computing equipment.   478

'Package' means a computer program or collection of programs   538
written for use by a number of people as opposed to one   593
written and tailored for a specific purpose or client.   647

'Program' means a set of instructions written in computer   704
language and carried out by the computer in sequence. Used   763
as a verb, the term 'program' means to write these instructions.   827

'Software' is the term used to describe the program - or set   887
of instructions - entered into the computer.   931

```
           5|    10|   15|   20|   25|   30|   35|   40|   45|   50|   55|   60|   65|
```

(SI = 1.56)

3 The alphabetic and numeric keyboard

TO BEGIN

Paper:	A5 landscape (210 x 148 mm).
Backing sheet:	Place a heavy-quality sheet of paper behind the top sheet to protect the cylinder/platen.
Line spacing:	1 (single).
First typing line:	7 lines from the top of the paper.
Margins:	Left hand—20 pica, 30 elite Right hand—not required (move to the extreme right).
Copy:	Copy each line at least twice. Space twice after each group of lines.
Errors:	If you make a mistake, continue keying. It is natural to make mistakes at first. Aim to improve your accuracy and your speed gradually.
Learning each new key:	Follow the steps given below before you practise the reach to a new key: 1 Locate the new key on your keyboard 2 Look at your fingers as you practise the reach to the new key 3 Without looking at your fingers, reach to the new key 4 Be sure that you can move from a guide key to a new key and back without looking before you type a new character 5 Refer constantly to the keyboard chart to review the location of the keys.

MAINFRAME, MINI AND MICROCOMPUTERS

5| 10| 15| 20| 25| 30| 35| 40| 45| 50| 55| 60| 65| strokes

A mainframe computer is a large, expensive machine which needs   62
many operators, programmers and analysts to be in attendance   122
when it is functioning. The modern mainframe computer is a   181
very powerful machine which can handle the vast volumes of   239
work generated by some large companies. The use of the com-   299
puter can be shared by a number of people who each have their   360
own terminal and who buy computer time. Mainframe computers   420
are also used for very complex calculations.   464

A mini computer is a small less expensive machine. It usually   527
needs the services of no more than a couple of specialists.   586
It has less power and storage capacity than the mainframe com-   648
puter, but the power at its disposal is sufficient for a wide   709
range of commercial and scientific applications.   757

A microcomputer is much smaller and cheaper again - so cheap,   818
in fact, that a large number of individual users can afford   877
to have their own machine.   903

5| 10| 15| 20| 25| 30| 35| 40| 45| 50| 55| 60| 65|

(SI = 1.6)

UNIT 1A

Guide keys
A S D F J K L ;

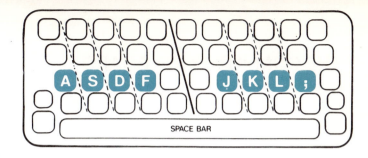

Position your fingers on the guide keys as shown on page 9.

Strike **F** and **J**	1	fff jjj fff jjj fff jjj fff jjj fff jjj
Strike **D** and **K**	2	ddd kkk ddd kkk ddd kkk ddd kkk ddd kkk
Review **F J D K**	3	fj fj dk dk fj fj dk dk fj fj dk dk fjf
	4	ff dd jj kk ff dd jj kk ff dd jj kk fff
Strike **S** and **L**	5	sss lll sss lll sss lll sss lll sss lll
Strike **A** and **;**	6	aaa ;;; aaa ;;; aaa ;;; aaa ;;; aaa ;;;
Review **S L A ;**	7	sl sl a; a; sl sl a; a; sl sl a; a; sls
	8	ss aa ll ;; ss aa ll ;; ss aa ll ;; sss
Review **A S D F ; L K J**	9	asdf ;lkj asdf ;lkj asdf ;lkj asdf ;lkj
	10	aa ss dd ff ;; ll kk jj a; sl dk fj a;a

THE COMPUTER KEYBOARD

| 5| 10| 15| 20| 25| 30| 35| 40| 45| 50| 55| 60| 65| strokes

The computer keyboard is similar to the keyboard of a type- 59
writer but has extra, specialised keys. Some of these extra 119
keys are outlined below. 143

The 'return' or 'enter' key is used to enter a program line or 205
a command after it has been typed and has appeared on the 262
screen. 269

The 'cursor control' keys are used to move the cursor around 329
the screen. The cursor is the marker which shows the position 391
on the screen where the next character you type will appear. 451

The 'break' key interrupts a program while it is running and 511
enables you to run it again or continue programming. 563

The 'delete' key enables you to erase the character you have 623
just typed on the screen if you have made a mistake. 673

Other keys on the keyboard have functions which are explained 734
in the user guide which comes with the machine, and there is 794
usually some provision for adding extra functions, depending 854
on the operator's requirements. 885

| 5| 10| 15| 20| 25| 30| 35| 40| 45| 50| 55| 60| 65|

(SI = 1.45)

UNIT 1B

CHECK THE POSITION
OF YOUR FINGERS
FOR KEYING BY TOUCH

Review

1   aaa ;;; sss lll ddd kkk fff jjj aaa ;;;
2   aa ;; ss ll dd kk ff jj aa ;; ss ll ddk

Word building

3   j ja jaf jaffa jaffas;
4   a as lass; alas a lass;
5   a ad lad lads; sa salad;
6   as ask lask flask flasks;

Sentence practice

7   a lad asks
8   add a jaffa
9   dad asks all
10   a jaffa falls
11   alf adds a salad
12   alas a flask falls

COMMON USES OF WORD PROCESSORS

5| 10| 15| 20| 25| 30| 35| 40| 45| 50| 55| 60| 65|	strokes

```
There are many uses to which a word processor can be put in      59
addition to typing.  This article outlines two of the more com- 122
mon ones, in which some of the special facilities of the word  183
processor are put to use.                                      208

In the typing of contracts in legal work, you need key in only 270
once all the clauses you might ever use, give each a name or   330
number, and save them on disk.  When you need a contract, all  391
you do is specify (in order) the name or number of the clauses 453
you need, and the word processor will automatically retrieve   513
them from the disk and assemble them into a document, appro-   573
priately numbered.  You can then make changes before printing  634
the final contract.                                            653

When keying a column of figures, the decimal tab key can help  714
you by lining up the decimal points, while a built-in calcu-   777
lator can let you double-check all rows and column totals and  835
percentages.                                                   847
```

5| 10| 15| 20| 25| 30| 35| 40| 45| 50| 55| 60| 65|

(SI = 1.43)

UNIT 2A

H E

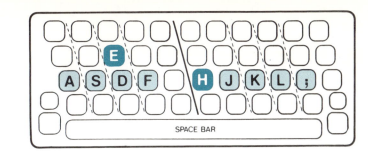

Review

Reach to **H**
Use **J** finger

Reach to **E**
Use **D** finger

Review **H** and **E**

1 a s d f j k l ; a s d f j k l ; a s d f
2 fj fj dk dk sl sl a; a; fj fj dk dk sls

3 jhj hhj jhj has has jhj had had jhj haj
4 jhj hall hall jhj half half jhj hash jh

5 ded eed ded eel eel ded eke eke ded elf
6 ded eeh ded eej ded eek ded eel ded ee;

7 he heal heal he head head he held held;
8 ha hake shake; sh she shed shell shells
9 a shelf; a sheaf; a shah; a sea; a seal
10 sea sea shell shell; she has sea shells

15

MAIN PARTS OF A COMPUTER

		strokes
5| 10| 15| 20| 25| 30| 35| 40| 45| 50| 55| 60| 65|		

All computers, whatever their size, consist of four basic parts.   64
These parts are: input devices, a memory, a central processor   126
and output devices.   145

Input devices take in data and convert it in one way or another   208
into the code which the computer can cope with. An input device   272
might be a switch, a keyboard or a microphone, and a computer   333
could have one or more of these devices.   373

The memory stores data, as well as the commands which have been   436
given to the computer. The commands are called programs.   493

The central processor acts as the 'brain' and processes the data   556
according to the program of commands.   594

Output devices receive messages from the computer and act on   654
these messages. Such devices include a TV screen (or visual   714
display unit - VDU) and a printer.   746

5\| 10\| 15\| 20\| 25\| 30\| 35\| 40\| 45\| 50\| 55\| 60\| 65\|

(SI = 1.55)

80

UNIT 2B

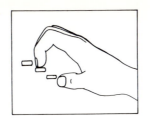

CHECK HANDS AND ARMS

Review

1 asdf ;lkj dede jhjh asdf ;lkj dede jhjh
2 hake hake jeff jeff sake sake feel feel
3 as ash ashes ashes; as ask asked asked;

Word building

4 ee eel heel heels
5 sh sha shake shakes
6 le lea leash leashes

Sentence practice

7 he has seals
8 he held a sale
9 a lad had a desk
10 a lessee had a lease
11 she shall sell a shed
12 della shall sell leeks

COMPUTERS TODAY

	strokes
In one way or another, we are all affected by computers in our	62
daily lives. Among other things, computers are used to make	122
travel bookings, to produce bank statements, to print various	183
types of accounts, to keep control of stock in stores, and to	244
provide a number of services in the home.	285
It is certain computers will become more widely used, and they	347
are already accepted as an essential part of modern business.	408
Thus, a knowledge of how they work and what they do is very	467
important.	477
It is important, too, to have a knowledge of computer terms.	537
The passages contained in this part of your book aim to help	597
you to understand some of the common computer terms and basic	659
computer concepts.	678

(SI = 1.46)

UNIT 2C
3

Review

1 asdf ded ;lkj jhj asdf ded ;lkj jhj asd
2 deed deed keel keel leek leek jess jess
3 jhhj heel heel heed heed hell hell jhhj

Reach to **3**

Use **D** finger

4 de3d d33d d33d 33 desk; 33 deed; 33 d3d
5 fad 3 had 3 jad 3 lad 3 jed 3 led 3 fed
6 leah has 33; jake had 33; jedda had 33;

Consolidate

7 jeff sees lee;
8 fae asked sasha;
9 jake sells shells;
10 kaja shall sell 33;
11 hess had 3 fake deeds;

WHAT IS A COMPUTER?

| 5| 10| 15| 20| 25| 30| 35| 40| 45| 50| 55| 60| 65| strokes

Computers are time-saving devices geared to simplify our lives   62
and our work. It is best to think of computers as our servants: 126
after all they do only what we tell them to do.   173

To operate a computer, you simply put data into the machine.   233
This data is stored in the computer, and you retrieve it when   294
you require it. A computer can be seen as a type of filing   353
system, but with a much more efficient means of finding infor-   415
mation.   422

It is possible today to enter a retail store and buy a desk-   482
top computer for the price of a colour television set. And,   542
since a computer is not much larger than the size of an aver-   603
age television set, it can be carried in the boot of a car to   664
the home or office.   683

| 5| 10| 15| 20| 25| 30| 35| 40| 45| 50| 55| 60| 65|

(SI = 1.41)

78

UNIT 3A

T I

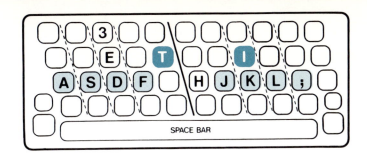

Review

1   aj ak al a; de he aj ak al a; de he aj;
2   ded ded; jhj jhj; ded ded; jhj jhj; ded

Reach to **T**
Use **F** finger

3   ftf ttf hat hat ftf jat jat ftf let let
4   ftf jest jest ftf that that ftf the the

Reach to **I**
Use **K** finger

5   kik iik ike ike kik ida ida kik tie tie
6   kik kite kite kik hilt hilt kik sit sit

Review **T** and **I**

7   iik ttf hit hit kit kit lit lit kii ftt
8   tied tied tiff tiff tilt tilt this this
9   fits fits lilt lilt tile tile diet diet
10 the list; the tide; the site; the thief

18

WHAT IS A WORD PROCESSOR?

													strokes
5|	10|	15|	20|	25|	30|	35|	40|	45|	50|	55|	60|	65|	

A word processor is a computer which is designed specifically — 61
to work with text. By text we mean letters, words, paragraphs — 123
and documents, etc. While a computer is a general-purpose — 181
machine, a word processor is used for text only. — 229

It should be noted that a word processor is much more than an — 290
advanced typewriter. Two features distinguish a word processor — 353
from an advanced typewriter. — 381

With a word processor, you can make substantial alterations — 440
to a text on a screen before it is printed, without having to — 501
retype the whole text. Further, text can be stored for future — 563
use. This means that if you need to use the text again, it — 621
does not have to be retyped. — 649

| 5\| | 10\| | 15\| | 20\| | 25\| | 30\| | 35\| | 40\| | 45\| | 50\| | 55\| | 60\| | 65\| |

(SI = 1.42)

UNIT 3B

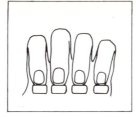

CHECK YOUR KEYSTROKING

Review

1 ded ded kik kik ftf ftf jhj jhj ded kik
2 ed ik tf hj ed ik tf hj ed ik tf hj ed;
3 jess jessie let lettie taff taffie till

Sentence practice

4 let the flats
5 fit this skate
6 this is the site
7 teddie is a thief
8 tessa hid the tiles
9 she tied these kites
10 the date is the fifth
11 he has the title deeds
12 hilda still has the kite

USES OF COMPUTERS

| 5| 10| 15| 20| 25| 30| 35| 40| 45| 50| 55| 60| 65| strokes

The uses to which computers can be put appear to be unlimited.　　62
As well as their use for business and domestic purposes, they　　123
can be used for playing games.　　153

Many games involve objects moving very fast across the screen.　　214
Games such as chess involve a great deal of calculation on the　　276
part of the computer.　　297

Educational games that are designed well can help students to　　358
develop their thinking.　　381

Business games are quite popular in management studies. The　　441
student is given all the information to enable him or her to　　501
make decisions about how to run a business. 'Chance' events　　561
like a fire, or sudden changes in commodity prices or interest　　623
rates, can be built in.　　646

| 5| 10| 15| 20| 25| 30| 35| 40| 45| 50| 55| 60| 65|

(SI = 1.53)

76

UNIT 3C

5 8

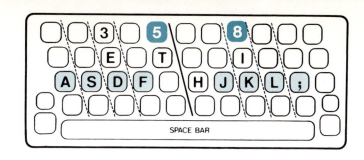

Review

1 asdf fttf ttft deed eede ;lkj jhhj hhjh
2 deft left sift haft kite kits kilt kids
3 d33d 33 edie 33 edit 33 elks 33 ekes 33

Reach to 5
Use F finger

4 ft5f t55f t55f 55 ties 55 take 55 tiff;
5 it 5 hit 55 fit 55 sit 55 kit 55 lit 55
6 ted let 5; tess jails 5; heidi takes 55

Reach to 8
Use K finger

7 ki8k k88k k88k 88 kit 88 ike 88 ilk 88;
8 teak 88 leak 88 desk 88 disk 88 task 88
9 the 88 skiffs sail; the 8 kites failed;

Consolidate

10 kissed kissed fitted fitted eddie eddie
11 th th kith kith that that this this the
12 the 88 kites; the 33 desks; the 55 ties

7 Passage drills

The format, content and scoring of the following passages are in accordance with the Australian Standard for Typing Speed Tests (Standard No 2708 – 1984).

- Key the following passages either timed or untimed.
- Do not key the figures to the right of the passages. These indicate a running score of the number of strokes keyed on completion of each line.
- Use A4 paper.
- Leave a top margin of six line spaces.
- Use 10-pitch type.
- Set the left-hand margin at 10. You may follow the copy line for line.
- If the passage is timed, the title is not to be included as a part of the timing.

CALCULATION OF SPEED

- Count the number of strokes keyed.
- Divide the total number of strokes by 5 to give the number of *standard typing words* completed.
- Divide this number by the number of minutes allowed for the test and correct it to one decimal place. The result represents typing speed in standard typing words per minute.

CALCULATION OF PERCENTAGE ACCURACY

- For your speed to be accredited or certified, it must be typed with at least 98 per cent accuracy, ie not more than two errors in every 100 standard typing words.
- The percentage accuracy is calculated by the following formula and then rounded to one decimal place.

$$\text{Percentage accuracy} = \frac{\text{standard typing words} - \text{errors}}{\text{standard typing words}} \times \frac{100}{1}$$

Example 1 — 250 standard words with *three* errors

$$\text{Percentage accuracy} = \frac{250 - 3}{250} \times \frac{100}{1}$$
$$= 98.8 = \text{PASS at that speed}$$

Example 2 — 250 standard words with *six* errors

$$\text{Percentage accuracy} = \frac{250 - 6}{250} \times \frac{100}{1}$$
$$= 97.6 = \text{FAIL at that speed}$$

UNIT 4A

R N

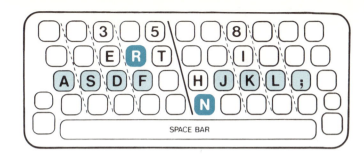

Review

1 ded kik ftf jhj ded kik ftf jhj ded kik
2 aia sia dia fia hia jia kia lia eia tia
3 tia tis tid tif ti; til tik tij tih tie

Reach to **R**
Use **F** finger

4 frf rrf rife rife frf rift rift frf rid
5 frf frisk frisk frf friar friar frf rrf

Reach to **N**
Use **J** finger

6 jnj nnj nits nits jnj nail nail jnj nil
7 jnj ran ran jnj hen hen jnj ken ken jnj

Review **R** and **N**

8 rrf nnj inn inner dinner sinner thinner
9 ent rent tent ear near dear earn learn;
10 dear sir; dear nan; dear ken; dear rina
11 frf jnj ren rend render ten tend tender

21

Water is more essential to life than food is; man can survive for only a few days without it. Water is needed for the functioning of all organs of the body. Sixty to seventy per cent of the body is water.

In many firms a career is built on job progression. This means that you learn to master one task before moving on to the next. On-the-job training is a continuous process which starts on your first day of work.

Walt Disney was a man who always liked to draw. The first time he made money out of his talent was when he drew a sketch of the horse belonging to a neighbour in his home town in Missouri. He was, then, a long way from his later success.

If you watch horse racing, motor racing or the runners and athletes who compete in the big events that are shown on television, you will know that the winners are the ones with the stamina to stay to the end as well as the great power necessary to speed ahead at the finishing line.

Chinese water deer and Asian musk deer do not have antlers. Except for the reindeer and the caribou, all female deer are without antlers. Deer shed their antlers once a year and then grow a new set. Hinds gnaw those that are discarded and hunters collect them as souvenirs.

UNIT 4B
TIMED WRITINGS

Calculate your keying speed on the basis of gross words per minute (GWPM) as follows:
- Count every five strokes (including spaces) as one word. (A word scale, marked in 5-stroke groups, is shown at the bottom of review lines, sentence practice and paragraph practice pieces which can be used for timed measures. One 'stroke' has been allowed for each return of the carriage or type element.) If you key three or more characters of your final word, count it as a complete word.
- Divide the number of words keyed by the length of the timing; for example, one minute.

Review

1 frf frf jnj jnj ftf ftf kik kik ded jhj;
2 nine and three are; three are this near;
3 jeni had a flat; heidi tested the train;
    1| 2| 3| 4| 5| 6| 7| 8|

Sentence practice

4 he said he heard
5 ira learns faster
6 her friend is fine
7 trish and rita think
8 renie had three friends
9 erina and triena are here
10 ken shall find her near here
    1| 2| 3| 4| 5| 6|

Paragraph practice
(Key this paragraph in single line spacing.)

11 he said that he heard janet thank karina near here; karina thinks that her friend is fine and has seen her in the theatre;
    1| 2| 3| 4| 5| 6| 7| 8|

Japan is a country of three thousand three hundred islands. There are four main islands and it is on these that the great majority of the huge population lives.

Do not do your work well simply in the hope of being commended. Always do your best for the sake of what you can put into your job, not for what you can get out of it.

The average adult does not read much faster than a child can read - about two hundred and fifty words per minute - but can absorb what is read at least twice as fast.

Camping still attracts the hardy type of person who seeks close contact with nature, but most people take it up because it enables them to enjoy the open air at low cost.

If a file is not returned to its right place in the cabinet, a lot of time may be wasted by someone who is looking for it. Filing is not difficult, it simply requires care.

Wedding rings are said to have originated from the custom of sealing a business transaction with a ring. Giving or exchanging rings was a sign of a contract well and truly made.

You should bear in mind that a letter may be the first contact that a client or customer has with your firm. The quality of the letter, therefore, gives an all-important first impression.

UNIT 4C

4

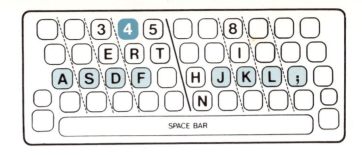

Review

Reach to 4
Use F finger

Consolidate

1 asdf ;lkj dee frr ftt jhh jnn kii fr jnn
2 fr fran jn jean ft fits de dens ki kink;
3 e33d 33d t55f 55f i88k 88k 38 55 38 555;
   1| 2| 3| 4| 5| 6| 7| 8|

4 fr4f f44f f44f 44 fine 44 felt 44 fires;
5 fair 44 hair 44 jeer 44 leer 44 near 44;
6 fran fired 44; ned hired 444; erna is 44

7 ft trill trent fr rent rest de erin ends
8 jn janet jenni ki kilns kirks jh jahada;
9 rrtt dirt shirt skirt flirt inert alert;
10 tter latter hatter natter sitter fitter;
11 nellie and athena and tina had fair hair
12 3 dens and 5 ties and 8 kids and 4 fires
   1| 2| 3| 4| 5| 6| 7| 8|

When you fly in an aeroplane and look out along the wing, you can see no sign of the forces that are lifting the plane into the air.

A secretary should be able to see what has to be done without being told. You should do all you can to make office life run smoothly.

Gold does not tarnish. Bells do not rust. And although silver may blacken, it can be polished until it shines as it would if it were new.

If you keep a list of phone numbers that you call often, check the numbers as soon as you receive your copy of the new telephone directory.

Make sure the postcode is on all postal items you or your staff send out. Show a return address on all posted articles that leave your office.

The attraction of music is a strong one for most people. It seems that we all have an inherent love of rhythm and the pleasant repetition of sound.

People who aim to have successful careers should direct their training and studies towards the particular types of job for which they are best suited.

UNIT 5A

C O

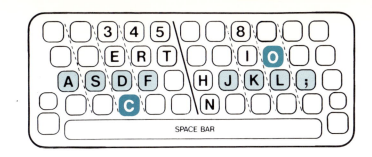

Review

1 frf jnj ftf kik ded jhj frf jnj ftf kik;
2 de dean fr fret tr trad je jean ki kind;
3 tanner tanner kerrie kerrie teller tells
   1| 2| 3| 4| 5| 6| 7| 8|

Reach to **C**
Use **D** finger

4 dcd ccd cede cede dcd ceil ceil dcd ccd;
5 dcd chic chic dcd cane cane dcd cats cat

Reach to **O**
Use **L** finger

6 lol ool old old lol oar oar lol one one;
7 lol lord lord lol lock lock lol lot lot;

Review **C** and **O**

8 co code co core co colt lo load lo loft;
9 on con non or for nor co coe cot no not;
10 the coin the coal the coat the cost the;
   1| 2| 3| 4| 5| 6| 7| 8|

24

Make every effort to find out all you can about job vacancies in the area in which you want to work.

The minutes of a meeting are a brief but clear record of the business transacted at that meeting.

A contract is an agreement made between two or more persons and is enforceable in a court of law.

When you are with a group of people, do not talk about topics which are not of interest to everyone.

Photos have many uses. They can be taken to look at, to record things, to show things or just for fun.

Filing is the storing of letters and other documents so that they can be found easily when required.

Take care of the words you speak, for they may do a lot of good or a lot of harm but they cannot be recalled.

The person who opens the mail in an office should take care not to cut any of the contents when slitting the envelopes.

The protein of milk is as good as the protein of meat and fish. It is superior to the protein of vegetables and cereals.

UNIT 5B

CHECK YOUR
SPACE BAR OPERATION

Review

1   dcd ded lol frf ftf kik jhj jnj dcd lol;
2   as df de dc fr ft ;l lo ki jh jn as df ;
3   lo loaf ce cent tr trod ce cell hi hides

    1| 2| 3| 4| 5| 6| 7| 8|

Sentence practice

4   order the locks
5   cecil can choose
6   corrie lent cora nine
7   john called at the store
8   the store is near cook lane
9   ronnie and carol jones joined leo
10   connie liked the coon cheese she tasted;

Paragraph practice

11   the date to close the tenders is set for the third; cath cannot alter it; she did intend to set a different date to close;

    1| 2| 3| 4| 5| 6| 7| 8|

A cheque is a bill of exchange drawn on a bank and payable on demand.

Steam rising from beneath the bonnet of a car is a sure sign of trouble.

At one time the games of bowls and golf were thought to be played only by old men.

Chess taxes the mind, and the one who is not alert is sure to be the one who will lose.

The ability to make a clear concise summary is a valuable asset in an office worker.

Show zest in your tasks day by day; take pride in all you do, big or small as it may be.

Always keep paper and a pencil by the side of the telephone so that you can take messages.

Every person who occupies any kind of position should have a keen sense of responsibility.

The human eye sees everything upside down and presents an inverted picture to the brain.

UNIT 5C

9

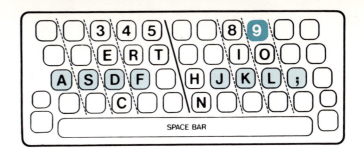

Review

Reach to 9
Use L finger

Consolidate

1 a s d e d c f r f t j h j n k i l o a s;
2 de dc decal; fr lo frock; fit jn fronts;
3 and 333 for 444 net 555 ock 888 3 4 5 88

  1| 2| 3| 4| 5| 6| 7| 8|

4 lo91 1991 1991 lock 99 loan 99 loft 999;
5 oslo 99 solo 99 oleo 99 halo 99 kilo 999
6 lola is 9 on the 9th and erica is 9 too;

7 echo decor cedar shock knock ikons john;
8 tion notion lotion ration action diction
9 ed canned netted jotted knotted trotted;
10 3 track 8 train 9 trier 5 trill 4 treats

  1| 2| 3| 4| 5| 6| 7| 8|

6 Paragraph drills

The paragraphs in this section are designed to:
- consolidate keyboard skills
- introduce the keyboard operator to the typing of passages.

To key the paragraphs
- Use A5 landscape paper.
- Leave a top margin of six line spaces.
- Set the left-hand margin at 10 pica, 18 elite.
- Move the right-hand margin to the extreme right.
- Use single-line spacing.
- Operate the line spacer/carriage return twice between each paragraph.
- Type each paragraph line for line.

UNIT 6A

FULL STOP
SHIFT KEYS

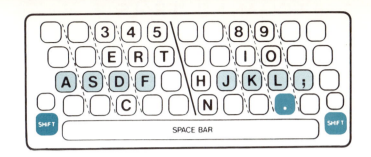

Review

Reach to **full stop**

Use **L** finger

Reach to **left shift key**

Use **A** finger

Sentence practice
Space twice after a full stop between sentences.

1   lol dcd jnj frf kik ftf jhj ded lol dcd;
2   d e d c f r f t j h j n k i l o a ; s l;
3   jinks heron cried adorn trick feels has;
    1| 2| 3| 4| 5| 6| 7| 8|
4   1.1 lock 1.1 lots 1.1 loan 1.1 loss 1.1.
5   1.1 for 1.1 off 1.1 hot 1.1 cot 1.1 oak.

To capitalise a letter keyed with a finger of the right hand, eg **H**:
- Position the **F** finger over the **F** key as you hold down the *left shift key* with the **A** finger. Now strike the **H** with the right-hand finger.
- Release the *left shift key* and return the **A** finger to the **A** key.

6   hHa jJa kKa lLa iIa nNa oOa hHa jJa kKa.
7   Iris Kath Lola Hesta Nella Oscar Janice.

8   Nada can. Linda does. Jill Harris ran.
9   Heidi and Nonie tried. Karen Nairn can.
    1| 2| 3| 4| 5| 6| 7| 8|

UNIT 30 ROMAN NUMERALS

Roman numerals are expressed by letters of the alphabet in either upper or lower case; for example, 'one' is expressed by upper or lower case 'i' in roman numerals.
(Arabic figures are: 1, 2, 3, 4, etc)

1 Upper case roman numerals for 1-6:   I, II, III, IV, V, VI.
2 Lower case roman numerals for 7-11: vii, viii, ix, x, xi.
3 Upper case roman numerals for 13-16: XIII, XIV, XV, XVI.
4 Lower case roman numerals for 18-21: xviii, xix, xx, xxi.

5 Do not use roman numerals in measurements: 1200 x 2000 m.
6 Do not use roman numerals when typing dates: 23 May 1982.
7 Do not use roman numerals when typing columns of figures.
8 Do not use roman numerals in ordinal numbers: 51st, 25th.

9 Page 34, Chapter IV; pages 340-461, Section III; Henry VIII.
10 King William IV; 11th July, 1911, World War II; Chapter XIX.
11 Act VI, Scene vii; Curlew II; Form IV; Stages I, II and III.
12 George VI died in 1952 and Elizabeth II was crowned in 1953.

68

UNIT 6B

Review

Reach to **right shift key**

Use   finger

Sentence practice

Paragraph practice

**CHECK YOUR
KEYING BY TOUCH**

1   1.1 dcd lol frf jnj ftf kik ded jhj 1.1.
2   1.1 Jane 1.1 Jack 1.1 John 1.1 Jean 1.1.
3   It is here. Lock the cars. Lend these.
     1| 2| 3| 4| 5| 6| 7| 8|

To capitalise a letter keyed with a finger of the left hand, eg **E**:
- Position the **J** finger over the **J** key as you hold down the *right shift key* with the **;** finger. Now strike **E** with the left-hand finger.
- Release the *right shift key* and return the **;** finger to the **;** key.

4   fF; dD; sS; eE; rR; tT; aA; fF; dD; cC;.
5   Freda; Donna; Sarah; Connie; Eric; Rona;

6   Elise and Terrie chose Delia and Cissie.
7   Tell Rosa and Sean that Cath told Erica.

8   Sandra and Annie told Tessa and Christie
    that this old car had an old seat in it.
     1| 2| 3| 4| 5| 6| 7| 8|

UNIT 29 SUPERIOR CHARACTERS
PART A

Alphabet review	1	equate lively fizzed magpie beckon jester expire hawker read
Common words	2	I can/I was/I had/I may/I know/I will/I made/I would/I have.
Numbers	3	She ordered 567 texts, 489 novels and 102 reference binders.
Signs and symbols	4	20 L barrels in containers 60.3 m x 74.5 m weighed 453.2 kg.
Paragraphs	5	After keeping the crowds in suspense, the explorers answered many questions about their amazing adventures in the jungle.

1| 2| 3| 4| 5| 6| 7| 8| 9| 10| 11| 12|

PART B

Key metric units	6	Your allotment measures 4 ha, but mine measures only 1 ha.
	7	The doctor said the dose should be 16 mL after every meal.
To key a superior character, turn back a half line space, key the superior character. Return to keying line.	8	The big house measured 230 m^2 with a swimming pool 80 m^3.
	9	I posted a letter weighing 25 g and a parcel weighing 2 kg.
	10	A full stop does not follow a metric symbol unless it is at the end of a sentence: 237 m 458 km, 936 ha, 19 L, 38 kg.
	11	Singular and plural forms are represented by the same symbol: 1 m, 7 m, 1 g, 6 g, 1 km, 3 km, 1 L, 9 L.

UNIT 6C

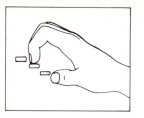

CHECK HANDS AND ARMS

Review

1 asd Dee Kii Dcc Jhh Frr Loo Ftt L.. Jnn.
2 eEE iII cCC nNN tTT oOO rRR iII aAA sSS;
3 333 and 444 and 555 and 888 and 999 ;;;;
    1| 2| 3| 4| 5| 6| 7| 8|

Consolidate

4 ft Tania lo Older jn North ki Ickle Ike.
5 jh Harah de Eric dc Cath fr Rick ft Ted.
6 Janet and Hannah and Freddie and Fitton.
7 ie fried cried dried kerrie nellie lies;
8 fttf totter totals titles tenets tartan.
9 Lettie had ten tickets for the theatres.
10 dcc confer contra corked circle chorals.
11 Credit Cecilie. Cart three cold crates.
12 Joe sailed. Kerin tried. Alice nodded.
    1| 2| 3| 4| 5| 6| 7| 8|

UNIT 28 METRIC, DEGREE°
PART A

Alphabet review	1	quaint awhile fizzes bright combed jovial expert yellow keys
Common words	2	only/if only/they can only/if it is only/which will only be.
Numbers	3	12 yesterday; 34 today; 56 tomorrow; 78 always; 900 any time
Signs and symbols	4	The sums were: 16 x 12 x 27 + 134 = ? and 56 x 12 - 189 = ?
Paragraphs	5	The exhausted traveller was pleased when a kind girl offered him a quiet place where he could rest and enjoy the breeze.

1| 2| 3| 4| 5| 6| 7| 8| 9| 10| 11| 12|

PART B

Key metric units	6	Her height was 178 cm and her weight was 72.5 kg.
	7	Buy 600 mL of orange juice and 2 L of peach nectar.
	8	There are two sizes: 1.85 x 2.75 m and 2.76 x 3.80 m.
To key a degree sign, turn back a half line space and key a lower case o. Return to keying line.	9	It was a very small box, being only 9.5 x 3.9 x 4.8 cm.
	10	The temperature was 14°C in Aberdeen and 16°C in Perth.
	11	She drove at 95 km/h to be in time for the 1500 m event.

UNIT 6D

BLOCK CAPITALS
1 With the little finger press the shift lock which is located above one or both of the shift keys
2 Key the word or words to be capitalised
3 Release the shift lock by pressing one of the shift keys.

PRACTICE
Key the following lines, remembering to release the shift lock by pressing a shift key when a capital is no longer required.

    1 `THINK AND LEARN FAST.`

    2 `HE ORDERED TEN LOCKS.`

    3 `JANE thanked FIONA and DANA for their loan.`

UNDERSCORING (UNDERLINING)
1 Locate the underscore symbol on your keyboard
2 Key the word/words to be underscored
3 Return to the first character to be underscored
4 Press the shift lock and underscore the word/words
5 Release the shift lock by pressing one of the shift keys.

PRACTICE
Key again the practice lines given above. Underscore all words that are capitalised.

UNIT 27 MULTIPLICATION, EQUAL SIGNS
PART A

Alphabet review	1	zipper motive warble pander squash joyful galaxy hockey webs
Common words	2	They can tell her soon if they are unable to do it for them.
Numbers	3	Trains will leave at 6.44 pm, 7.33 pm, 8.55 pm and 10.22 pm.
Signs and symbols	4	Find the answers to these two sums: $15 \div 5 + 6$; $9 \div 3 + 10$.
Paragraphs	5	There was joy in his family when Ken won the expensive prize for growing the best quality vegetables in the district.

1| 2| 3| 4| 5| 6| 7| 8| 9| 10| 11| 12|

PART B

Reach to Multiplication sign (use lower case x)	6	**Practise the reach to** x
	7	216 x 18 and 126 x 52 and 1023 x 9 and 323 x 144.
	8	Calculate the following: 948 x 20 and 8634 x 50.
Reach to equation sign	9	**Practise the reach to** =
	10	93 − 3 = 90; 378 − 100 = 278; 9147 − 3526 = 5621.

UNIT 7A

Y W

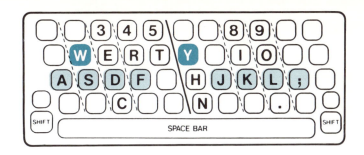

Review

1 1.1 lol dcd ded jnj jhj frf ftf kik 1.1.
2 1.1 Fill; 1.1 Dole; 1.1 Jars; 1.1 Hails.
3 Claire or Kath or Jeff or Des or Janice.
   1| 2| 3| 4| 5| 6| 7| 8|

Reach to **Y**
Use **J** finger

4 jyj yyj yah yah jyj yet yet jyj yen yen.
5 jyj yells yells jyj yacht yacht jyj yes.

Reach to **W**
Use **S** finger

6 sws wws was was sws wan wan sws wad wad.
7 sws walk walk sws word word sws win win.

Review **Y** and **W**

8 weary weary worry worry carry carry cry.
9 few few new new law law jaw jaw saw saw.
10 ty tyre cy cyst ly lyre ry ryot ey eyes.
   1| 2| 3| 4| 5| 6| 7| 8|

UNIT 26 PLUS, DIVISION SIGNS
PART A

Alphabet review	1	prized moving wanted buckle jingle queens theory whiffs vex.
Common words	2	In time he will be able to do more than they are able to do.
Numbers	3	8 per day; 4 per week; 2 or 3 per year; 67 to 90; 815 times.
Signs and symbols	4	Rosen, Bloome & Co Ltd, Cnr Bathurst & Kent Streets, Sydney.
Paragraphs	5	He was subject to frequent attacks of dizziness and so could not be expected to climb the very high mountain range.

1| 2| 3| 4| 5| 6| 7| 8| 9| 10| 11| 12|

PART B

Reach to plus sign	6	Practise the reach to +
	7	12 + 34; 56 + 78; 90 + 21; 43 + 65; 87 + 9; 5 + 8
	8	Add together 4 + 6 + 9. Add together 8 + 17 + 5.
Reach to division sign by keying the minus sign, backspacing, and keying a colon.	9	John exclaimed, "Show the calculation as 15 ÷ 5!"
	10	Divide the number of units by 12 thus: 144 ÷ 12.
	11	Show your calculations thus: 300 ÷ 10; 132 ÷ 11.

64

UNIT 7B

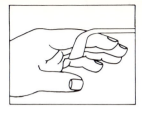 

CHECK YOUR LINE SPACING

Review

1 jy jh jn fr ft ki de dc ki sw lo l. sws.
2 Read the data. File the disks. It was.
3 Strike a key. Read your screen. It is.
    1| 2| 3| 4| 5| 6| 7| 8|

Sentence practice

4 They wore woollen yarn.
5 Software was on sale last year.
6 Yenda will try to ride the cycle.
7 Wyn had two new white cars last year.
8 Ronny went to work at <u>York</u> on <u>Wednesday</u>.
9 <u>Wendy Gray</u> wanted to work for two years.
10 Rory said Troy Yow was the winner today.

Paragraph practice

11 This narrow road was the shortest way to the water. Wayne reached the water when he went on his way to the northern town.
    1| 2| 3| 4| 5| 6| 7| 8|

UNIT 25 &, MINUS SIGN
PART A

Alphabet review	1	froze jumpy whirl house quiet kinky guava limbs toxic laden.
Common words	2	to which/to them/to that/to what/to have/to her/to the/to do
Numbers	3	2nd-5th February, 6th-9th March, 3rd-7th April. 4th-8th July
Signs and symbols	4	Shirts @ $16.00 and skirts @ $10.00 were seen in the <u>Herald</u>.
Paragraphs	5	Just as the sun was coming over the horizon the next day, we picked up our bags and resumed our quest for the gold.

1| 2| 3| 4| 5| 6| 7| 8| 9| 10| 11| 12|

PART B

Reach to ampersand	6	**Practise the reach to &**
	7	1 & 0 and 2 & 9 and 3 & 8 and 4 & 7 and 5 & 6 and
	8	Messrs Row & Co, Messrs Yee & Co, Messrs Low & Co
Reach to minus sign (use the hyphen)	9	**Practise the reach to –**
	10	5656 - 565 and 4747 - 474 and 3838 - 838 and 2929
	11	Calculate the following: 135 - 79 - 16 - 14 - 12.

63

UNIT 7C

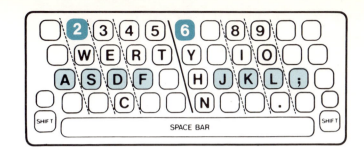

2 6

Review

Reach to **2**
Use **S** finger

Reach to **6**
Use **J** finger

Consolidate

1   sws ded dcd frf ftf jyj jnj kik lol 1.1.
2   swell decks frets forts hands kiwis joy;
3   ice 3 fir 4 jet 5 kik 8 woo 9 die 34589.
    1| 2| 3| 4| 5| 6| 7| 8|
4   sw2s s22s s22s 22 sway 22 seen 22 sorts.
5   cow 22 how 22 row 22 new 22 jew 22 stew.
6   Wayne is 22. Gwyn saw 2. Yew sold 222.

7   jy6j y66j y66j 66 jars 66 jaws 66 joins.
8   hay 66 jay 66 kay 66 coy 66 roy 66 ways.
9   Katy ate 6. Rory had 66. Faye saw 666.

10 Sww Sweeney Jyy Jerry Loo Lotty Ftt Tia
11 There were 66 away on 22 June last year.
    1| 2| 3| 4| 5| 6| 7| 8|

UNIT 24 @, UNDERSCORE
PART A

Alphabet review	1	telex julep giver lunch fuzzy moist queer pride break lowly.
Common words	2	on it/on the/on you/on that/on your/on them/on this/on which
Numbers	3	11 boys 27 girls 38 bunnies 49 bubbles 50 cattle 61 bottles.
Signs and symbols	4	He/she can pay between $1000 and $6000 for his/her holidays.
Paragraphs	5	Would you please remove the cracked jugs from the box and so prevent the liquid from oozing onto the table.

1| 2| 3| 4| 5| 6| 7| 8| 9| 10| 11| 12|

PART B

Reach to **at** sign

6 Practise the reach to @

7 let @ sew @ pan @ rug @ but @ now @ mow @ both @.

8 1 frock @ $105, 1 brown suit @ $99, 1 shirt @ $9.

Indicate italics by underscoring

9 Practise the reach to the underscore

10 Inspect my stock of china, pottery and glassware.

11 We shall travel by bus, train or ferry if we can.

62

UNIT 8A

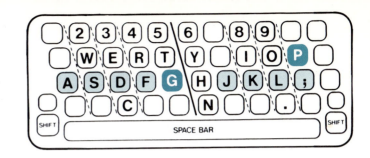

G P

Review

1 fr ft jyhnj dedcd ki sw lol.l fr ft jyjn
2 far jet yes nan eye ice kit soy low had.
3 Card files. Daisy wheels. Coded words.
   1| 2| 3| 4| 5| 6| 7| 8|

Reach to G
Use F finger

4 fgf ggf gaff gaff fgf golf golf fgf gay.
5 fgf figs figs fgf grit grit fgf gig gig.

Reach to P
Use ; finger

6 ;p; pp; pep pep ;p; pay pay ;p; paw paw.
7 ;p; prey prey ;p; page page ;p; pig pig.

Review G and P

8 petty pretty; party parity; poddy podgy.
9 ght ght sight fight light nights rights.
10 pi pin pipe pick pint gr grey grip grow.
   1| 2| 3| 4| 5| 6| 7| 8|

34

UNIT 23 DOLLAR SIGN, DIAGONAL/SOLIDUS
PART A

Alphabet review	1	gauze vexed peeps right beams knock jewel filly quell heaps.
Common words	2	there had/there will/there were/there have/there would/there
Numbers	3	56 themes; 565 folios; 5665 departures; Nos 656, 556 and 665
Signs and symbols	4	Sale! Sale! Some stock reduced by 10%, other stock by 15%.
Paragraphs	5	A long queue of excited parents gave a joyous welcome to the athletes who brought back the prized medals.

1| 2| 3| 4| 5| 6| 7| 8| 9| 10| 11| 12|

PART B

Reach to dollar sign	6	**Practise the reach to $**
	7	$10, $20, $30, $40, $50, $60, $70, $80, $90, $100
	8	Pay $1.00, $9.00, $2.00, $8.00, $37.50 or $36.50.
Reach to diagonal/solidus	9	**Practise the reach to /**
	10	bit / men / are / fan / win / per / ice / yards /
	11	Order No 115/32 and Invoice No 129/203 were sent.

61

UNIT 8B

CHECK YOUR SHIFT KEY TECHNIQUE

Review

1 rf tf gf yj hj nj ed cd ik sw ol .l ;p;p
2 Flap; Slap; Crop; Prop; Whip; Grip; Nip;
3 Page endings. Page display. Page nine.
   1| 2| 3| 4| 5| 6| 7| 8|

Sentence practice

4 Greg and Pia Gray agreed to sign a page.
5 Peter opened the shop near Paget Parade.
6 Pip Parke is flying to Port Perry again.
7 Peggy and Glenda saw eighty people play.
8 Gerry grasped the edge of the torn page.
9 Pack and wrap the present in pink paper.

Paragraph practice

10 Greta and Peg are going to Perth for the gala parade and concert. They will stay one week in Sydney on their way if Peter Greene agrees to store their cases away.
   1| 2| 3| 4| 5| 6| 7| 8|

UNIT 22 EXCLAMATION MARK, PER CENT
PART A

Alphabet review	1	apex jury bear kilt evil moan foal heed quiz lace glow kiss.
Common words	2	and is/and the/and were/and have/and they/and what/and which
Numbers	3	Telephone 47 4477; 147 River Street, Revesby; 744 varieties.
Signs and symbols	4	She said 'Have you read "The Eye of the Storm" yet?'. 'No'.
Paragraphs	5	Terrie and her friends used a wide jet of foam to quench the blaze and extinguish the fire very quickly.

1| 2| 3| 4| 5| 6| 7| 8| 9| 10| 11| 12|

PART B

Reach to exclamation mark. Space twice after an exclamation mark at the end of a sentence.	6	**Practise the reach to !**
	7	How heavy the rain is! How glad the farmers are!
	8	"Stop, thief! Stop, thief! Catch him, someone!"
Reach to per cent	9	**Practise the reach to %**
	10	and % for % peg % off % yet % mob % her % jets %.
	11	50% profit; 25% tax; 10% discount; 5% commission.

60

UNIT 8C

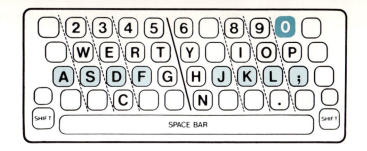

0

Review

1 sw de dc fr ft fg jh jy jn ki lo l. ;p;p
2 fgf girl goat gift ;p; ping prong prigs.
3 is 2 he 3 or 4 it 5 eh 6 di 8 so 9 is 2.
   1| 2| 3| 4| 5| 6| 7| 8|

4 ;p0; ;00; ;00; paw 00 pat 00 pay 00 pan.
5 code fp000; part gp000; code cp000; 000;
6 20 pears; 30 pigs; 40 years; 50 peaches;

Reach to 0
Use ; finger

Consolidate

7 fr frown rogue rajah jn nicks naked neat
8 ft fitch trait trite jy yacht yelps yell
9 dc cocoa cools codes sw swags swore wigs
10 ;p props perry peaks lo loose lotto logs
11 ppP ggG nnN wwW kkK eeE iiI ssS jjJ aaA;
12 50 kg of grapes or 2 kg of pepper; 3 kg;
   1| 2| 3| 4| 5| 6| 7| 8|

UNIT 21 APOSTROPHE, QUOTATION MARKS

PART A

Alphabet review	1	deaf joke grab lack zoom open vase yarn whip ibex aqua tents
Common words	2	he would/ it would/ we would/ they would/ when would/ these would
Numbers	3	38th place; 338 students; 38c and 83c each; 883 times; 8338;
Signs and symbols	4	Today (of all days) she will visit Como* (if it stays fine).
Paragraphs	5	The kind teacher jumped over the wooden fence and gazed most anxiously at the quarrelling boys.

  1| 2| 3| 4| 5| 6| 7| 8| 9| 10| 11| 12|

PART B

Reach to double inverted commas/ quotation marks	6	Practise the reach to "
	7	All news was published in "The Warringah Weekly".
	8	"If I feel well," she said, "I shall leave soon".
Reach to single inverted commas/ apostrophe	9	Practise the reach to '
	10	'May I borrow "Gulliver's Travels"?' he asked me.
	11	The child's toys; the man's house; the boy's dog.

59

UNIT 9A

U Q

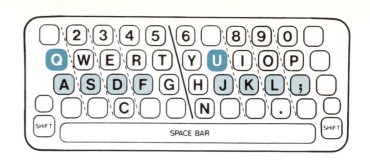

Review

1   fgftf jhjyj swsws ;p;p; dedcd lol.l fgfg
2   ws ed cd rf tf gf hj yj nj ik ol .l ;p;p
3   Copy this page. Changes in type styles.
    1| 2| 3| 4| 5| 6| 7| 8|

Reach to U
Use J finger

4   juj uuj jug jug juj jut jut juj rug rug.
5   juj jury jury juj judo judo juj uke uke.

Reach to Q
Use A finger

6   aqa qqa quay quay aqa quad quad aqa qua.
7   aqa quips quips aqa query query aqa quo.

Review U and Q

8   qui quick quiet que queue quests quench.
9   ruin ruck ruth rust pure cure lure sure.
10 quack quaff quirk urges units usage use.
    1| 2| 3| 4| 5| 6| 7| 8|

UNIT 20 PARENTHESES, ASTERISK
PART A

Alphabet review	1	crow jump gave lazy taxi huge barn like turf mass quay mends
Common words	2	he is/and is/now is/she is/what is/that is/this is/which are
Numbers	3	9.29 am on Thursday; 29th February; 92nd copy; 229 arrivals;
Signs and symbols	4	Co-ordination and co-operation are required--at least today.
Paragraphs	5	Janelle was puzzled by the quantity of very old garments she found when she unlocked the box.

1| 2| 3| 4| 5| 6| 7| 8| 9| 10| 11| 12|

PART B

Reach to parenthesis	6	Practise the reach to (and)
	7	ten (10), eleven (11), twelve (12), thirteen (13)
	8	The typewriters (priced below cost) are bargains.
Reach to asterisk	9	Practise the reach to *
	10	As the sun rose, MacDonald** sighted land to port
	11	** Captain Dougal MacDonald, 1712-1780.

UNIT 9B

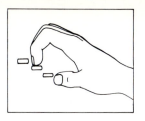

CHECK HANDS AND ARMS

Review

1 aqa ;p; sws lol ded kik frf juj ftf jyjy
2 quilt creek knelt foggy windy units sups
3 Quit now. Use a quill. Quaff your tea.
    1| 2| 3| 4| 5| 6| 7| 8|

Sentence practice

4 Request a quote for yellow quarto paper.
5 He was required to quit the quarry site.
6 This quest for opals had a happy sequel.
7 Enquire whether that quota was required.
8 He asked us to quieten the short queues.

Paragraph practice

9 They required quite a high grade of work for entry in this quest. She shall plan to work quickly and quietly so that each of the products is the highest standard. She knows that she has to start quickly.
    1| 2| 3| 4| 5| 6| 7| 8|

UNIT 19 HYPHEN, DASH
PART A

Alphabet review	1	best helm dame jack quit oxen wick love from haze grip yelps
Common words	2	and have/ can have/ will have/ they have/ which have/ should have
Numbers	3	Item No 101; 10 pm on Wednesday; 101 copies; No 10 platform;
Signs and symbols	4	Will they? Can we? They are: red, purple and white. Why?
Paragraphs	5	The man requested his friends to walk along the zigzag paths just beyond the excavations.

1| 2| 3| 4| 5| 6| 7| 8| 9| 10| 11| 12|

PART B

Reach to hyphen	6	Practise the reach to -
	7	My well-to-do-friend tried to co-operate with me.
	8	In the 1982-83 report pages 192-208 were omitted.
Key a dash	9	The dash is keyed correctly--at last--as you see.
(note the two methods of keying a dash)	10	The dash - which denotes a pause - gave emphasis.

UNIT 9C

1 7

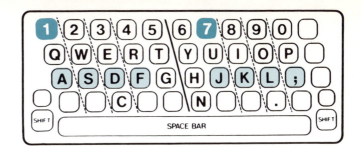

Review

1	aq aqua sw swig de deal fr frog ft fits.
2	fg fogs dc dice jn nape ju juke jy eyes.
3	s2 d3 f4 t5 y6 k8 i9 ;0 23 34 45 56 89 0

1| 2| 3| 4| 5| 6| 7| 8|

4	aqla alla alla ll ape ll aid ll aye ll a
5	ll quills ll queens ll quests ll quoits.
6	Prue sold ll quires of paper on ll June.

Reach to 1
Use **A** finger

Reach to 7
Use **J** finger

7	ju7j j77j j77j 77 jug 77 jut 77 jan 777.
8	77 jigs 77 joys 77 jets 77 jaws 77 jest.
9	There were 777 people in 777 new queues.

Consolidate

10	ng wing ring king ck knock quack trucks.
11	Judy sent 7 jugs on 17 June and 27 July.

1| 2| 3| 4| 5| 6| 7| 8|

UNIT 18 QUESTION MARK, COLON
PART A

Do not key the dividing strokes

Alphabet review	1	farm host verb yawn camp next quip mill gaze jute lame docks
Common words	2	do the/if the/to the/of the/as the/for the/was the/were they
Numbers	3	f55f j66j f44f j77j d33d k88k s22s 1991 alla ;00; 564738291;
Signs and symbols	4	Irma, Iris, Isla, Eric, Ella, Erie; Ross, Ruby, Rory, Renie;
Paragraphs	5	Jackie is both lax and lazy and her work may require a great deal of supervision.

1| 2| 3| 4| 5| 6| 7| 8| 9| 10| 11| 12|

PART B

Reach to question mark. Space twice after a question mark at the end of a sentence.	6	**Practise the reach to ?** – see sample drill on page 55.
	7	Are you? Have they? What is? Can she? Was it?
	8	May she go? Was it typed? Will they travel yet?
Reach to colon. Space twice after a colon.	9	**Practise the reach to :**
	10	This is the address: 8 Oceania Street, Cape Ray.
	11	This is what I did: I paused, I turned, I cried.

UNIT 10A

B COMMA

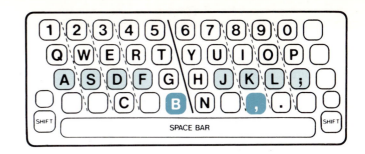

Review

Reach to **B**
Use **F** finger

Reach to **comma**
Use **K** finger

Review **B** and **,**

1   fgf frf ftf jhj juj jyj sws lol aqa ;p;p
2   aa qq ;; pp ss ww ll oo ff rr jj uu ggff
3   was rip jet fig hay nod kit all quo cop.
    1| 2| 3| 4| 5| 6| 7| 8|
4   fbf bbf bid bid fbf bus bus fbf bar bar.
5   fbf bows bows fbf buff buff fbf bat bat.

6   k,k ,,k pick, pick, k,k back, back, k,k,
7   k,k bright, bright, bought, bought, k,k,

8   bi bile, ba bale, fa fables, bu bubbles,
9   ca cabby, sq squib, bo bones, br brands,
10 Bebe, Toby, Robby, Pete, Ruby and Bruce.
    1| 2| 3| 4| 5| 6| 7| 8|

5 Signs and symbols

The drills in this section are designed to:
- review keyboarding skills
- teach the reaches to punctuation signs, symbols and miscellaneous signs and give you practice of them
- show the correct method of keying metric units
- show the correct method of keying roman numerals.

Each unit is divided into two parts.

Part A contains the following types of drill:
1 an alphabet review
2 common words
3 numbers
4 signs and symbols
5 paragraphs.

Part B contains drills on new signs or symbols. As these signs or symbols may be located in different positions on different keyboards, you should:
1 Locate each character on your keyboard.
2 Decide which finger to use for each key; for example, if the dollar sign ($) is on the 4 or 5 key, use the F finger.
3 Practise the movement and correct stroking technique for each character by keying it and the corresponding guide key letter, for example:

```
f4f  f$$f  f4f  f$$f  f4f  f$$f  f4f  f$$f
```

INSTRUCTIONS

Paper: A5
Margin: 10 pica, 20 elite
Spacing: Single
- Key each line two or three times.
- Turn down two single line spaces after each group of lines.

UNIT 10B

CHECK YOUR KEYSTROKING

Review

1 aqa ;p; sws lol ded kik frf juj ftf jyj;
2 fgf jhj fbf jnj dcd k,k l.l fbf jnj dcd,
3 ture, nature, suture, capture, lectures,
   1| 2| 3| 4| 5| 6| 7| 8|

Sentence practice

4 The big, blue books are in this library.
5 Bob, Barb, Bert and Brady were betrayed.
6 A tab bar can be used for typing tables.
7 Business was buoyant, which is pleasing.
8 The business was bought by her brothers.

Paragraph practice

9 The book, bought as a guide, was used by business people and their clients. This book is bound with beige and bright blue fabrics. The quality was beyond belief. This book, we know, has been used often.
   1| 2| 3| 4| 5| 6| 7| 8|

UNIT 17

0
DECIMAL POINT

Warm up

Reach to **0** and **.**
Use thumb for **0**
Use third finger for **.**

Review **0, 1, 2, 3,
4, 5, 6, 7,
8, 9, .**

1 474 414 585 525 696 6366 4714 5285 6936
2 747 141 858 252 969 3633 4174 5825 6396

3 404 505 606 040 050 0600 4000 5000 6000
4 6.6 .66 6.6 .66 6.6 6.66 66.6 6.66 66.6
5 40.6 50.6 60.6 46.6 56.6 66.6 40.6 50.6
6 67.6 68.6 69.6 67.6 68.6 69.6 67.6 68.6

7 101 202 303 404 505 6.60 7.60 8.80 9.90
8 .10 .20 .30 .40 .50 6.00 7.00 8.00 9.00

54

UNIT 10C

CHECK YOUR SPACE BAR OPERATION

Review

1   aa bb cc dd ee ff gg hh ii jj kk ll nnn.
2   oo pp qq rr ss tt uu ww yy aa bb cc ddd.
3   11, 22, 33, 44, 55, 66, 77, 88, 99, 000,

Consolidate

4   ftft jyjy frfr juju dede kiki swsw lolo.
5   aqaq ;p;p dcdc k,k, fbfb jnjn 1.1. 1.1.1
6   fbbf bubble babies baboon bibles bobbed;
7   Bobby Brown broke the bright blue bowls.
8   aqla 11 air sw2s 22 swabs de3d 33 dates.
9   fr4f 44 fry ju7j 77 judge t55t 55 trips;
10 y66j 66 yak ki8k 88 keels lo91 99 lobes.
11 ;p0; 00 ponds 10, 29, 38, 47, 566, 1000.
12 Code No 223, Part No 4455, Item No 6677.
13 10 April 1985, 29 June 1974, 3 February,

UNIT 16

9 3

Warm up

Reach to **9** and **3**
Use third finger

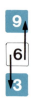

Review **1, 2, 3, 4,
5, 6, 7, 8,
9**

1   456   456   585   585   525   525   5825   7515   88   22
2   654   654   858   858   252   252   5285   1575   85   25

3   69   69   6996   96   96   9696   69   69   6996   96   969
4   63   63   6336   36   36   3636   63   63   6336   36   363
5   6963   3639   9636   3663   3993   6993   6336   6936
6   6369   9369   9699   3633   6939   9366   3966   9933

7   69   63   59   49   53   43   969   363   619   6796   6316
8   96   36   98   32   93   39   896   236   343   7896   1236

UNIT 11A

M X

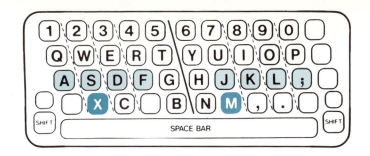

Review

Reach to **M**
Use **J** finger

Reach to **X**
Use **S** finger

Review **M** and **X**

1 fbf jnj ftf jyj dcd k,k sws lol aqa ;p;p
2 ab cd ef gh ij kl no pq rs tu wy ab cd e
3 Ask Billy to hire Wendy a car in Quebec.
   1| 2| 3| 4| 5| 6| 7| 8|

4 jmj mmj mug mug jmj mud mud jmj mum mum;
5 jmj music music jmj jumps jumps jmj jam;

6 sxs xxs six six sxs sox sox sxs lax lax.
7 sxs boxed boxed, sxs fixed fixed, proxy,

8 mo mopes mi mixes mu mural ma maple made
9 ex exam ex expo ho hoax ma manx wa waxy.
10 Dear Madam, Dear Mr Muir, Dear Mrs Marx,
   1| 2| 3| 4| 5| 6| 7| 8|

UNIT 15

8 2

Warm up

Reach to 8 and 2
Use second finger

Review 1, 2, 4, 5,
6, 7, 8

1 456 456 474 474 414 414 1456 4567 77 11
2 654 654 747 747 141 141 6541 7654 74 14

3 58 58 5885 85 85 8585 58 58 5885 85 858
4 52 52 5225 25 25 2525 52 52 5225 25 252
5 5852 2528 8525 2552 2882 5885 5225 5825
6 5258 8258 8588 2588 5825 8255 2855 8822

7 58 52 47 41 42 62 858 252 587 5214 5874
8 74 14 84 24 21 87 414 474 262 8685 2585

52

UNIT 11B

CHECK YOUR SPACING

Review

1   sxs 1.1 dcd k,k fbf jmj jnj sxs 1.1 dcdc
2   grunt bluff enjoy sweep hacks squid axle
3   Ask Max to rent Jacques a bike for July.

    1| 2| 3| 4| 5| 6| 7| 8|

Sentence practice

4   Lexy was lax in paying the excess taxes.
5   The exact excise was seen as an expense.
6   Mamie and Maxine Martens paid extra tax.
7   Myra and Mem tried to exhibit a lax air.
8   That excess should not exceed six cents.

Paragraph practice

9   The six exits were crammed many times as the excited crowd left the game. If you expect the six exits may clear some time soon, you can fix a time to go, and just relax for a while. Maxy soon came back.

    1| 2| 3| 4| 5| 6| 7| 8|

UNIT 14

7 1

Warm up

Reach to 7 and 1
Use first finger

Review 1, 4, 5, 6, 7

1 44 55 66 456 445 556 664 4656 4556 5664
2 45 56 65 546 665 554 446 6465 6445 6554

3 47 47 4774 74 74 7474 47 47 4774 74 747
4 41 41 4114 14 14 1414 41 41 4114 14 141
5 4741 1417 7414 1441 1771 4774 4114 4714
6 4147 7147 7477 1411 4714 7144 1744 7711

7 47 41 57 51 67 61 747 757 767 4747 4141
8 74 14 75 15 76 16 141 151 161 7474 1414

51

UNIT 11C

CHECK YOUR KEYING BY TOUCH

Review

1   dedc deacon frfr furry jujm jumper jyjnj
2   swsx saxe lol. logs kik, kick aqaq quit.
3   ftfb both y6 t5 u7 r4 i8 e3 o9 w2 p0 ql.

        1   2   3   4   5   6   7   8

Consolidate

4   me mends memos meant meets medals melons
5   ex exits exact exams exalt excel exerts.
6   br broom broke brown brims bride bright.
7   tty witty catty putty lotty jetty kitty.
8   ru rumps rumba rusks rules rugby rupees.
9   po pole post pond port pots pokes poems.
10 th thick thief those threw there things.
11 ster master caster poster roster jester.
12 qu quest quote quick quart quads quells.
13 A train departs at 12.35 am or 12.47 pm.

        1   2   3   4   5   6   7   8

UNIT 13

Guide keys
4 5 6

Strike **4, 5, 6**

1 44 55 66 44 55 66 44 55 66 44 55 66 444
2 45 45 56 56 46 46 45 45 56 56 46 46 455

3 444 555 666 444 555 666 444 555 666 444
4 464 564 545 464 564 645 464 564 645 464
5 5664 6445 5446 5564 6645 4465 4665 6554
6 5654 6546 4645 5456 6465 4546 5645 6564

7 66 54 46 565 546 645 646 5465 6454 4656
8 64 56 65 654 465 564 456 4565 5645 6546

UNIT 12A

V Z

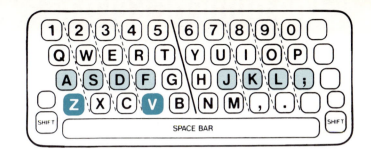

Review

1	frf juj ftf jyj fbf jnj fgf jhj jmj jnjn
2	sws lol sxs l.l aqa ;p; ded dcd kik k,k,
3	Find a daisy wheel or golf ball element.

1| 2| 3| 4| 5| 6| 7| 8|

Reach to **V**
Use **F** finger

4 fvf vvf via via fvf vet vet fvf vim vim.
5 fvf have have fvf nerve nerve fvf grove.

Reach to **Z**
Use **A** finger

6 aza zza zeal zeal aza zero zero aza zed.
7 aza quiz quiz aza jazz jazz aza liz liz.

Review **V** and **Z**

8 viv vice vice vi view view vo vows vows.
9 zez zebu zebu zi zips zips za zany zany.
10 one dozen, two dozen, three dozen, four.

1| 2| 3| 4| 5| 6| 7| 8|

46

4 The numeric keypad

The numeric keys are located above the alphabet keys on a standard keyboard (see the keyboard illustration on the front of the lift-out chart).

On many computer terminals a numeric *keypad* is provided, separate from the *keyboard* and located to the right of the keyboard (see the keypad illustration on the back of the lift-out chart). The numeric keypad usually includes the numbers 0 to 9, the decimal point, function keys and the enter key.

The keypad allows for the entry of numbers at a faster rate than is possible when working with the numeric keys above the alphabet keyboard. It is used when the material to be keyed consists largely of numeric data.

The material provided in units 13 to 17 will develop your skill in keying numbers on a keypad.

If you do not have a keypad on the machine which you are operating, use the lift-out keypad to practise the reaches to the various keys so that you can become familiar with this part of a computer.

KEYPAD INSTRUCTIONS

Place the first three fingers of the right hand on the keys 4, 5 and 6 which are the guide keys of the keypad. Reach to the keys above and below from this position. The keypad numbers do not always appear in the order shown on the lift-out illustration.

To space between groups of figures, strike the space bar with the thumb of the right hand. Use the little finger to strike the enter key at the end of each line.

The blank keys on the keypad illustration are provided for you to insert the function keys in the positions in which they appear on the machine you are operating. Practise the reach from the guide keys to each function key with the most convenient finger.

In the following exercises copy each line at least twice.

UNIT 12B

CHECK YOUR SHIFT KEY TECHNIQUE

Review

1 aqa aza kik k,k sws sxs juj jmj ;p; l.l.
2 abcdefghijklmnopqrstuvwxyz abcdefghijklm
3 gave, quit, haze, exit, mist, brow, fan,

    1| 2| 3| 4| 5| 6| 7| 8|

Sentence practice

4 The Gazebo Motel provides good services.
5 We availed ourselves of the vast ranges.
6 <u>Dave Zolton</u> and <u>Vera Zoro</u> were over age.
7 Zara saw a dozen amazing filing systems.
8 Zena avoided using Venice for the venue.

Paragraph practice

9 Their job was to seize five new computer programs. Dozens had tried before them; all had failed. She was dazzled by this obviously difficult job. She seized the programs contained on four floppy disks. The huge megabyte capacity puzzled them.

    1| 2| 3| 4| 5| 6| 7| 8|

UNIT 12C

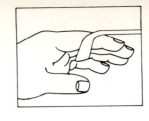

CHECK YOUR LINE SPACING

Review

1 abcdefghijklmnopqrstuvwxyz. abcdefghijk
2 jugs quiz back vows expo lady form hunt.
3 1a 2s 3d 4f 5f and 6j 7j 8k 9l 0; and 1a

The following lines give practice on letters of the alphabet as shown.

z 4 Lizzie saw the lazy boys seize a zither.
e 5 Evie says she eats three eggs every day.
q 6 Your questions quickly caused a quarrel.
x 7 Maxie and Tex expect to catch six foxes.
p 8 Paula had pork chops, peas and potatoes.
m 9 Mark mailed the memo to Mrs Moore today.
v 10 The heavy mist covered the vast valleys.
b 11 Bobbie brought a big box of brown bread.
t 12 Tony travelled by taxi, train and truck.
w 13 Wally Weldon was too weary to work well.